JOAN MIRO

The Potato. 1928. Oil on burlap, 39⅝ x 32⅛ inches. Private Collection, New York.

JOAN
MIRO

BY JAMES JOHNSON SWEENEY

THE LIBRARY
COLBY JUNIOR COLLEGE
NEW LONDON, N. H.

THE MUSEUM OF MODERN ART, NEW YORK

ND 6
813
M5
S9
Copy 1

25690

COPYRIGHT, 1941

THE MUSEUM OF MODERN ART, 11 WEST 53 STREET, NEW YORK CITY

PRINTED IN THE UNITED STATES OF AMERICA

CONTENTS

ACKNOWLEDGMENTS

The President and Trustees of the Museum of Modern Art and the Director of the Exhibition, James Johnson Sweeney, wish to thank those who have lent to the exhibition and, in addition, those who have generously rendered assistance: A. Everett Austin, Jr.; André Breton; Leslie Cheek, Jr.; W. G. Constable; Mr. and Mrs. Chester Dale; Miss Katherine S. Dreier; William N. Eisendrath; A. E. Gallatin; Paul G. Gardner; William Stanley Hayter; Thomas Laughlin; André Masson; Pierre Matisse; Roland J. McKinney; Mme. Pilar Juncosa de Miro; Dr. Grace L. McCann Morley; Gerald Murphy; Luis Sert; Mrs. Florence Stol; Gordon Washburn.

LENDERS TO THE EXHIBITION

Mr. and Mrs. Walter C. Arensberg, Hollywood; Mrs. Cornelius N. Bliss, New York; Mr. and Mrs. Henry Clifford, Radnor, Pa.; Mme. Marie Cuttoli, New York; The Chester Dale Collection, New York; Mrs. Valentine Dudensing, New York; Miss Valentine Dudensing, New York; A Conger Goodyear, Old Westbury, N. Y.; Mrs. George Helm, New York; Mrs. H. Gates Lloyd, Haverford, Pa.; Dr. and Mrs. Leslie M. Maitland, West Los Angeles; Mr. and Mrs. Pierre Matisse; Peter, Paul and Jack Matisse, New York; Mrs. Saidie A. May, Baltimore; Henry McBride, New York; Mr. and Mrs. C. Earle Miller, Downingtown, Pa.; Mme. Helena Rubinstein, New York; Pierre Matisse

Gallery, New York; Nierendorf Gallery, New York; Valentine Gallery, New York; Albright Art Gallery, Buffalo; Wadsworth Atheneum, Hartford; The Société Anonyme Collection, Yale University; Museum of Living Art, New York University, New York.

TRUSTEES OF THE MUSEUM

Stephen C. Clark, *Chairman of the Board;* Wallace K. Harrison, *1st Vice-Chairman;* Samuel A. Lewisohn, *2nd Vice-Chairman;* John Hay Whitney, *President;* David McAlpin, *Treasurer;* Alfred H. Barr, Jr., *Vice-President and Director;* John E. Abbott, *Executive Vice-President;* Mrs. Robert Woods Bliss, Mrs. W. Murray Crane, Marshall Field, Edsel B. Ford, Philip L. Goodwin, A. Conger Goodyear, Mrs. Simon Guggenheim, Mrs. David M. Levy, Henry R. Luce, Archibald MacLeish, William S. Paley, Mrs. John Parkinson, Jr., Mrs. Charles S. Payson, Mrs. John D. Rockefeller, Jr., Beardsley Ruml, Carleton Sprague Smith, Edward M. M. Warburg.

HONORARY TRUSTEES: Frederic Clay Bartlett, Frank Crowninshield, Duncan Phillips, Mrs. Rainey Rogers, Paul J. Sachs, Mrs. John S. Sheppard.

STAFF OF THE MUSEUM

Alfred H. Barr, Jr., *Director;* John E. Abbott, *Executive Vice-President;* Monroe Wheeler, *Direc-*

tor of Exhibitions and Publications; Frances Hawkins, Secretary; Ione Ulrich, Assistant Treasurer and Comptroller; Douglas L. Baxter, Production Manager; Elizabeth Litchfield, Assistant to the Director.

Department of Painting and Sculpture: Alfred H. Barr, Jr., Curator; Dorothy C. Miller, Associate Curator.

Department of Architecture: Janet Henrich, Acting Curator.

Film Library: John E. Abbott, Director; Iris Barry, Curator; Edward F. Kerns, Technical Director; Allen Porter, Circulation and Exhibition Director.

Department of Industrial Design: Eliot F. Noyes, Director.

Department of Photography: Beaumont Newhall, Curator.

Department of Exhibitions: Monroe Wheeler, Director; Carlos Dyer, Technical Assistant.

Department of Circulating Exhibitions: Elodie Courter, Director.

Department of Publications; Monroe Wheeler, Director; Holger E. Hagen, Manager.

Library: Beaumont Newhall, Librarian.

Publicity Department: Sarah Newmeyer, Director.

Department of Registration: Dorothy H. Dudley, Registrar.

Educational Project: Victor D'Amico, Director.

Information Desk: Ernest J. Tremp.

BRIEF CHRONOLOGY

1893   Born April 20 at Montroig, near Barcelona, Spain.

1907   Entered School of Fine Arts in Barcelona.

1910   As result of difficulties with his parents, gave up painting to work in an office.

1912   Entered Academy Gali, Barcelona, to resume painting.

1915   Left Academy Gali and began to paint on his own.

1917   Met Dalmau, a Barcelona art dealer, who had already begun to interest himself in the work of the cubists and the young Spanish painters.

1918   February 16 to March 3 first one-man show, Barcelona, organized by Dalmau. Sixty-four canvases and many drawings dating from 1914 to 1917.

1919   First visit to Paris, in March.

1920   Settled in Paris. Public demonstrations by dada group in Paris.

1921   Dalmau arranges one-man show in the Galerie La Licorne, Paris, April 29 to May 14. Preface to catalog written by Maurice Raynal. *Portrait of a Spanish Dancer*.

1922   Completed *The Farm*, which represents nine months' work; begun at Montroig, it was continued at Barcelona, then finished in Paris at 45 rue Blomet. A synthesis of the work of Miro up to this point.
June: Large international exhibition organized by orthodox dadaists at the Galerie Montaigne.

1923   *The Tilled Field*.

1924   *First Manifesto of Surrealism*, published by André Breton, defining surrealism.

1925   Exhibition at Galerie Pierre, Paris, arranged by Jacques Viot, June 12–June 27.
Exhibited with surrealists in first group exhibition, November.
Designs for costumes and settings for Diaghileff's Russian Ballet, *Roméo et Juliette* in collaboration with Max Ernst.

1926   Miro painting, *In Reverse*, first to be shown publicly in America, by the Société Anonyme: Museum of Modern Art: 1920, at the Brooklyn Museum.
March 10 *La Galerie Surréaliste* opens with exhibition including work by Miro.

1928   Visit to the Netherlands.
Publication of Breton's *Surréalisme et la peinture* describing Miro as "possibly the most surrealist of all of us."
First exhibition in America at Valentine Gallery, New York.

1930   Important exhibition of collages at Galerie Goemans, Paris, including work by Miro; preface to catalog by Louis Aragon entitled *Peinture au défi*.

1931   Designs for costumes and settings for Monte Carlo ballet *Jeux d'Enfants*.

1937   Large mural decoration for Paris Exposition.

1939   Withdrew from Paris to Varengeville-sur-Mer.

1940   Fall of France; returned to Barcelona, thence to Palma, Majorca.

1941   Palma, Majorca.

JOAN MIRO

GAIETY, sunshine, health—color, humor, rhythm: these are the notes which characterize the work of Joan Miro.

Joan Miro is above all else a painter. This is what distinguishes him from so many of his best known contemporaries. This is the key to his own stylistic evolution. This is the basis on which he has built the most revolutionary contribution made within the strictly pictorial form by any painter of the generation immediately following that of Pablo Picasso.

But Miro is also a poet. "What really counts," he has said, "is to strip the soul naked. Painting or poetry is made as we make love; a total embrace, prudence thrown to the wind, nothing held back." . . . "Have you ever heard of greater nonsense than the aims of the abstractionist group? And they invite me to share their deserted house as if the signs that I transcribe on a canvas, at the moment when they correspond to a concrete representation of my mind, were not profoundly real, and did not belong essentially to the world of reality! As a matter of fact, I am attaching more and more importance to the subject matter of my work. To me it seems vital that a rich and robust theme should be present to give the spectator an immediate blow between the eyes before a second thought can interpose. In this way poetry pictorially expressed speaks its own language." . . . "For a thousand men of letters, give me one poet!"[1]

These are the ideals which give Miro's work its character and have dominated his evolution as a painter. To follow his growth is to follow the pattern of his efforts toward embodying these ideals in his art. The need of Miro's generation was a recall of the imagination to painting. In combating the abuses which had derived from an exaggerated interest in the descriptive possibilities of painting, Miro's immediate seniors, the cubists and others, had gone dangerously far in the direction of denying those features any value whatsoever. The young men of the early 1920's recognized the importance of a renewed stress on spiritual values in painting.

This new romantic spirit, however, demanded a fresh field. Psychoanalytic research and the unfamiliar words of free, irrational association which it revealed, offered a suggestion. It was eagerly accepted. But in reacting against the cubists' exaggerated emphasis on formal fundamentals, many of the most talented surrealist painters forgot the lessons that the previous generation had learned. Miro, however, was an exception. Thanks to his almost all-exclusive interest in painting, he has been able to keep his finger on the benefits that the severe disciplines of the earlier generation had won, and at the same time meet the problem of his own generation with an equal or even greater effectiveness than any of his contemporaries. As André Breton, one of the founders of the surrealist movement, stated in its heyday: "There is, in Joan Miro, apparently only one interest, that of giving himself over entirely to painting, and only to painting, with that

[1] DUTHUIT, GEORGES. Où allez vous Miro? Cahiers d'Arts 11 no 8-10:261-264 1936.

13

pure automatism on which I for my part have never stopped calling, and of which Miro seems to have found out for himself, in short order, the sound value and good sense. Perhaps indeed on these grounds he may be regarded as the most thorough surrealist of all of us."[2]

In his work Miro is essentially a Catalan—that type of fantasist visionary which, in the Middle Ages, produced the manuscript illuminations of Beatus' commentaries on the Apocalypse—that mixture of oriental and occidental sympathies which made it possible for Raymond Lully, in the thirteenth century, to open up the vernacular to the paths of philosophy through exploitation of two cultures, Latin and Arabian, which existed side by side in the Catalonia of his day. Miro's color rarely offers the sombre tonalities we associate with so much Spanish painting particularly that of the great masters of the post-Renaissance, El Greco, Zurbaran, Velasquez and Goya. His has a blither note. In it there are echoes of the early provincial church decorators of Catalonia; frequently, the bold contrasts of yellows, blues, scarlets and greens of the Beatus backgrounds; throughout we feel the gay spirit of contemporary Catalonian folk art. Within the rhythms of his compositions the slow movements of a Spanish dance will suddenly burst into those of a Catalan Sardana with its intoxicating swing and wistful skirl of pipes.

Because of his fundamental devotion to painting, Miro has been able to recognize the value of the lessons learned by those generations immediately preceding his who sternly emphasized the formal bases of painting. Because he was a poet, he saw the weakness of a pictorial expression which discouraged any enrichment by means of extra-pictorial suggestion. Through the combination of these two sides of his talent, he has been able to bring a new tonic element into contemporary painting without compromising an essential pictorial approach. And the record of Miro's development to date is a history of the constant single-minded effort he has made toward combining and perfecting these abilities.

Joan Miro was born at Montroig, near Barcelona, on April 20, 1893. At the age of fourteen he entered the School of Fine Arts in Barcelona. He was not a quick pupil and his earliest efforts were discouraging to his parents. After three years they prevailed on him to give up art school for a position in an office. Between 1910 and 1912 Miro did no painting whatsoever. In 1912, however, he took it up again and entered the Academy Gali at Barcelona. Since 1915 he has devoted himself entirely to painting.

In Miro's early development an important role was played by the sympathetic insight of two of his first teachers. Urgell, his professor at the School of Fine Arts, was prompt to recognize certain qualities of Miro's self-contained nature. He encouraged the observant reflective side of Miro's character and fostered a natural contentment in solitude that distinguishes Miro even today. A later master, Pasco, Miro recalls, encouraged him to take every possible liberty necessary to finding his individual path, exerting pressure only in developing Miro's feeling for color.

[2] Breton, André. Le surréalisme et la peinture. Paris, Gallimard, 1928.

14

The Chauffeur. 1918. Oil on canvas, 26¾ x 24 inches. Collection Walter P. Chrysler, Jr., New York.

1912-1920

Nevertheless, when Miro entered the Academy Gali after two years' abstention from painting, he was in his own words "a phenomenon of clumsiness." "Color spoke to me," he says, "but as to form, I was a cipher. I was barely able to distinguish a straight line from a curve. I only succeeded in developing a sense of form through drawing after the sensation of touch—by feeling the shape of things with my eyes closed and then attempting to draw them."[3]

Miro's earliest work was a typical advanced art-school product of the period. This character gradually gave way, in landscapes such as the *Beach at Cambrils*,[4] to a clearly fauve approach, or more exactly a personal derivation from the manner of the fauves' own predecessor, van Gogh.

Very soon, however, a personal note began to appear. In *The Chauffeur* of 1918 (above) Miro shows a certain confidence in his technique, even though here the idiom inherited from van Gogh still sits on his forms like a borrowed suit. And with this first sense of ease we see a characteristic feature of his personality breaking through—that sly humor which was so often to fuse the pictorial elements of his later work into a fresh and individualized iconography.

In spite, however, of this first appearance of confidence in *The Chauffeur*, Miro's color interest still seemed to run away with his drawing; and there was still a distinct survival of the loose formal handling which had marked Miro's fauve landscapes of the year before. But in the *Landscape with Donkey* (page 16) of the same year we see an effort toward a richer, more complex composition. And in the canvases of 1919 such as the *Landscape with Olive Trees, Nude with*

[3] LEIRIS, MICHEL. Joan Miro. Documents no5:263-6 O 1929.
[4] CAHIERS D'ART 9no1-4:263 1934.

15

Landscape with Donkey. 1918.
Oil on canvas. Collection Pierre
Loeb, Paris.

Nudes. 1917. Pencil, 7¼ x 5⅞ inches and 7⅜ x 5⅝ inches. Private Collection, New York.

16

Landscape with Olive Trees. 1919.
Oil on canvas, 28½ x 35½ inches.
Pierre Matisse Gallery, New York.

Nude with Mirror. 1919. Oil on canvas, 44 x 40 inches. Pierre Matisse
Gallery, New York.

Self Portrait. 1919. Oil on canvas. Collection Pablo Picasso, Paris.

18

Mirror, and *Self Portrait* (pages 17 and 18), it is evident that Miro has realized the need to tighten and refine his expression. It is apparent from his two pencil drawings of 1917 (page 16) that Miro was aware even at that date of the disciplinary value of the cubist approach. In 1919 in the *Landscape with Olive Trees* and the *Nude with Mirror* he employed a personal interpretation of cubism as a means of strengthening the flaccid, stringy forms that characterized the bulk of his earlier work, just as he had worked in the van Gogh-fauve manner while developing his color sense. We need only compare his *Nude with Mirror* with *The Chauffeur* of the year before to see the result. And it is equally easy to see the new breadth of treatment by comparing the *Landscape with Olive Trees* with the earlier, perhaps more idyllic *Landscape with Donkey* from which it is so evidently a descendant. While the forms have become broader and more confident, the color, nevertheless, has lost nothing. Miro's tactile approach—his "sense of form through drawing after the sensation of touch"—may have given him a sounder sense of volumes, but it was not until he had mastered certain cubist fundamentals that he was able to translate his sense of physical relations into effective combinations of visual symbols. Then, in 1919, he pulled a tight skin over the volumes his cubist discipline had taught him to construct, with the result that the loose, expressionist forms of *The Chauffeur* and its predecessors were replaced by the firm structure of his well-known *Self Portrait*, at present in the collection of his fellow-countryman, Pablo Picasso.

Toward the end of 1917 Miro had made the acquaintance of Dalmau, a Barcelona art dealer who was interested in the work of the cubists and had begun to take up the younger Spanish painters. In 1918 Dalmau gave Miro his first one-man show in his gallery in Barcelona. The exhibition comprised sixty-four canvases and many drawings, all dating from 1914 to 1917. In 1919 Miro made his first trip to Paris. He arrived there in March and remained the winter. He returned to Spain the next spring. But the following winter found him back in Paris once more and, shortly afterward, installed in the rue Blomet studio of his countryman, Pablo Gargallo, who was then teaching in the School of Fine Arts in Barcelona.

1920-1925

In April of 1921 Dalmau organized Miro's first one-man show in Paris at the Galerie La Licorne under the sponsorship of the critic, Maurice Raynal, who contributed the preface to the catalog. Raynal liked Miro's work even at this early date. He and Picasso brought Paul Rosenberg to see him in the early months of 1921. Raynal thoroughly understood Miro's temperament and appreciated his audacities, which he felt were "never irritating." In fact he encouraged his rashness as a "source of those fertile errors which have so often illumined art." In the Paris show twenty-nine canvases and fifteen drawings dating from 1917 to 1920 were shown. Nothing was sold. For Miro a long period of hardship and poverty followed, which was to be brought to a close only by the sensational success of his exhibition at Pierre Loeb's gallery in the rue Bonaparte in 1925.

The period 1920–1925 was perhaps the most important in Miro's development. In it he was at first trying to perfect his technique; he satisfied his desire for objective representation in *The Farm*

Still Life with Rabbit. 1920. Oil on canvas. Collection Pierre Loeb, Paris.

(page 23); then he gradually broke down conventional forms into a more individual idiom; and finally, he achieved sufficient confidence to wipe his canvas bare for new explorations.

But it is not to be supposed that Miro undertook any of these steps in his evolution according to a conscious program. Even the changes from the loose fauve technique of his early years to that of his 1919 *Self Portrait* were more intuitive than reasoned. As he says himself, "It is always passion and faith which lead me on—I change my painting often in search of means of expression; it is always this burning passion which guides me, which makes me walk from left to right." This is undoubtedly true. Nevertheless, the line of his evolution is remarkably straight, much more direct probably than if it had been based on a reasoned criticism. Those strayings from right to left which he speaks of are only superficial. Out of the fanatic concentration, in his apprentice years, on perfecting his means of expression, his persistent effort to compose every picture as well as possible—to balance all the elements and harmonize the color and drawing—came a sense of pictorial rightness which guided him more effectively than any rationalization could.

At the same time another even deeper urge moved him. This was his desire to ally poetry with painting, to give a spiritual color, a suggestive quality to his pictures. He realized this could not be achieved so fully as he desired through the use of conventional descriptive forms.

Portrait of a Spanish Dancer. 1921. Oil on canvas. Collection Pablo Picasso, Paris.

21

In the important 1920 still lifes such as the *Still Life with Rabbit* (page 20), and in such works as the 1921 *Portrait of a Spanish Dancer* (page 21), is to be found the fullest development of Miro's objective self-discipline. Just as the *Landscape with Olive Trees* was a broadening and strengthening of the *Landscape with Donkey*, the *Still Life with Rabbit* is clearly an outgrowth of the lessons Miro learned through the *Landscape with Olive Trees*. And the *Portrait of a Spanish Dancer* in the same way offers a crispness of drawing and modeling that carries us along in technical achievement to the end of this phase of Miro's evolution and *The Farm* of 1921–1922.

All this, however, was primarily a sharpening of tools. And temperamentally Miro could not be satisfied with that alone. He wanted to be sure of his tools and confident in his idiom, but not solely for their own sakes. He wanted to be able to say something with them—not merely to describe something—completely, even scientifically. But strangely enough it was Miro's concentration on the objective world closest to him at this time that was eventually to serve as the bridge from a straightforward, craftsmanlike description of material models to a subjective world of association, sentiment and, finally, of fantasy.

That bridge was *The Farm* of 1921–1922 which Miro began to paint, *sur le motif*, at Montroig, continued in Barcelona, and finished in Paris after nine months of steady work, much hardship, and in the end undoubtedly many a nostalgic backward glance toward the original subject matter. This picture is the master-key to much of Miro's later development. It represents the objective source of long series of fantastic variations, both on its general theme and on elements selected from it, dating from its conclusion practically to the present day. Like Dublin to James Joyce in his continental exile, the homestead at Montroig where Miro was born served him as a base on which to build his fantasies and dreams far away in Paris. And we can see the persistent spell of this memory in the development, simplification and elaboration of references to *The Farm* that turn up in Miro's work, from the *Tilled Field* of 1922–1923 (page 27) through *The Family* of 1924 (page 32), *The Harlequin's Carnival* of 1924–1925 (facing page 32), the *Dutch Interiors* of 1928 (page 48) and the large 1933 *Compositions* (page 55), even down to 1940, when the Montroig rooster becomes the Gallic cock in a gouache prepared for the review *Verve*[5] just before the fall of France.

The Farm, in Miro's work, represents the close of his first period of discipline and the opening of the period in which he adapts his hard-won technique to new ends of expression. In *The Farm* we first find as great an interest in the subjective as in the objective. A poetry of sentiment, a nostalgia suffuses the picture. Robert Desnos, in describing Miro's studio in the rue Blomet that year, writes: "*The Farm* was the first of his pictures I saw. It lighted up his whole whitewashed studio. One wall was completely hidden by huge bare canvases. . . . It was a fine day. The sun gave the weedy, miserable court a lovely country charm. In one corner of the studio was a table covered with Balearic toys, little gnomes, strange animals in plaster illuminated in lively colors.

[5] VERVE. 11no8:77 S-N 1940.

22

The Farm. 1921–22. Oil on canvas, 52 x 58 inches. Collection Ernest Hemingway, Havana.

Flowers and Butterfly. 1922–23. Tempera on wood, 31¼ x 25½ inches. Collection Dr. and Mrs. Leslie M. Maitland, West Los Angeles.

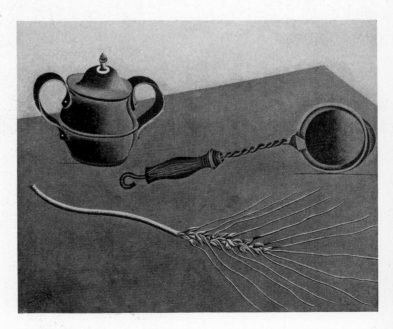

The Ear of Grain. 1922–23. Oil on canvas, 14⅞ x 18⅛ inches. The Museum of Modern Art, New York.

The Farmer's Wife. 1922–23. Oil on canvas, 31¾ x 25½ inches. Collection Pierre Matisse, New York.

These little creatures seemed to have come out of *The Farm*. They gave the studio a holiday, fairy-tale air, and I tried in vain to rack my brains for a memory of which I was only able to call back the ghost, the savor, so to speak—a childhood tale in which mushrooms played the principal roles."

The drawing in *The Farm* is as crisp as in the *Portrait of a Spanish Dancer* and the composition even denser than that of the *Still Life with Rabbit*. The colors have a cold austerity, with a curious relation to Spanish popular prints in their yellows, tobacco browns, blacks and greens. Every detail is worked out with meticulous care—every crack in the plaster, every leaf, every loose stone is painted as if it alone were important. Miro has made use of every variety of linear pattern from the moss-grown plaster of the barn, to the grain in the wood of the dovecote and the dog's foot-prints in the path. At the same time he has organized a rich pattern of related motifs built around the black circle at the foot of the central tree and the triangle of tiles beside it. We find every conceivable variation of each of these dominant forms throughout the picture. The circle is frankly repeated in the sun and the hen's nest and, elliptically, in the various pails and cans scattered about the farmyard. The triangle of the tiles is repeated immediately alongside in a black shadow, again in the gables of the barn and tool shed, then echoed throughout every corner of the canvas from the reflection of the chicken netting to the disused tiles in the extreme right foreground.

The Farm is a synthesis of Miro's objective interests up to that time. The few frankly objective studies that appear in 1922 and 1923, such as the flower still lifes (page 24), *The Ear of Grain* (page 24) and the *Carbide Lamp* are bits left behind in the cornucopia after *The Farm* had been poured out, rather than contributions toward a future culminating work.

The most important of these "fragments" from *The Farm* is the *Farmer's Wife* of 1923 (page 25), which broadens and simplifies certain rhythms and forms of the parent picture. Instead of the dominant black circle and triangle there is now a dominant white circle and triangle with variations in the black lines framing the woman and the black shape of the stove bottom. The grotesquely exaggerated feet, the elimination of depth and the generally more abstract style of the *Farmer's Wife* indicate Miro's direction. However, the broad simplicity of *The Ear of Grain* and the *Farmer's Wife* is temporarily forgotten in the works immediately following, to reappear as one of the dominant characteristics of Miro's style of the mid-1920's.

The Farm marks the beginning of a new interest in sentiment and associative suggestion—the poetic approach which is to play such an important role in his subsequent work. His next ambitious composition, *The Tilled Field*, of 1923–1924, again has the same nostalgic theme but treated with much greater freedom and less objective realism. Here we have a beginning of the elisions, the suggestive shorthand which is to characterize his idiom more and more. While *The Farm* was founded on observation and developed after the painter's eye had been withdrawn from the model, he approaches *The Tilled Field* through his associational memory rather than his visual memory. From now on he is no longer interested in how a scene actually looked; he is interested

The Tilled Field. 1923–24. Oil on canvas, 26 x 37 inches. Collection Mr. and Mrs. Henry Clifford, Radnor, Pa.

rather in that of which it reminds him. Instead of attempting to describe, he now sets about noting down these resemblances and suggestions. The result begins at once to take on the character of a pictorial metaphor rather than a representation. For example, in *The Tilled Field* he evidently cares less about the appearance of the scene than his awareness of the listening quiet, symbolized by the great ear, and the eyes watching him from every corner—the rural calm and the live animality he associates with Montroig.

This was one side of Miro's development. Two other important features were an increased abstraction of form and a greater complexity of compositional rhythms. *The Tilled Field* was a recognizable advance in abstraction; yet for all the formal exaggerations employed, the composition remains relatively simple. It is rather the *Catalan Landscape* (page 29) of the same year that marks a distinct advance in this direction. Here Miro's formal simplifications carry him in many instances to the barest of ideographs, most of them linear. At the same time, in keeping with general attenuation of forms we have a thinning of color—both in tone and in application—pale pinks, oranges and yellows, in contrast to the warm reds, greens, browns and blues of *The Tilled Field*—a light wash instead of the earlier thicker paint.

Up to this point Miro's growth seems mainly the outcome of changes within himself and consequent reinterpretations of the formal researches of his predecessors. With the *Catalan Landscape* we begin to see the influence of contemporary art movements around him in Paris. His incorporation of the letters S a r d, for example, has a clearly dadaistic character as a commentary on the subject matter. In *The Farm* and *The Tilled Field* he had employed fragments of the newspaper titles *L'Intransigeant* and *Le Journal*. But in those pictures they were used as in cubism. While the letters S a r d, still function as formal elements in the composition, they also play an extra-pictorial role. As an abbreviation of Sardana, the popular national dance of Catalonia, they suggest both the holiday spirit in which the picture should be approached and the associations it offered with the painter's native land. Again, in keeping with his nostalgia, we see his native flag linked with that of the country of his residence. The wheel and ladder motifs from *The Farm* reappear and we recognize the painter's palette in the lower left-hand corner. Sentiment gives Miro his theme, and his contacts with the dada movement give him an idiom for understatement and a certain mild self-mockery. The mustachioed figure smoking a pipe in the upper left-hand corner, probably intended as a self portrait, is a character which will reappear constantly during the next year and a half until its final appearance in *The Harlequin's Carnival*.

The long discipline which Miro's work on *The Farm* entailed, had burned it into his memory. It is not likely that distance diminished his sentimental feeling, but maturity undoubtedly refined it. Possibly this is why each new metamorphosis of a motive from *The Farm* grows less realistic, yet seems to carry with it a greater aura of suggestion. And with these changes of form and feeling there is a related change in color. The fact that the artist is no longer interested in description so much as in suggestion has produced a profound change in his total pictorial organization which

28

Catalan Landscape (The Hunter). 1923–24. Oil
on canvas, 25½ x 39½ inches. The Museum of
Modern Art, New York.

In Reverse (*Le Renversement*). 1924. Oil, pencil,
charcoal, tempera on canvas, 36¼ x 28⅜ inches.
Yale University, The Société Anonyme Collection.

Pastoral. 1923–24. Oil drawing on canvas, 23½ x 36 inches. Pierre Matisse Gallery, New York.

has already begun to turn away from a conventional central axis to an all-over disposition of flowing rhythms, as in the *Catalan Landscape.*

Ever since Miro's arrival in Paris he had been closely in touch with the younger men there, to whom his fellow-countryman Picasso had introduced him. Pablo Gargallo's studio, which he took over, was separated only by a thin partition from that of André Masson, one of the most active of the younger generation of painters conscious of a need to find a way from the cubism of his predecessors to a more emotional expression. There, as Desnos described it,[6] "many of the younger poets and writers were accustomed to gather"—Georges Limbour, Fraenkel, Leiris, Salacrou, Viot and others.

The air was full of controversy and new ideas. In 1920 the dadaists gave their first public demonstration in Paris at the Palais des Fêtes. Poems were read, music played and sculpture and painting exhibited—notably Duchamp's LHOOQ (Mona Lisa with a mustache)—which aroused considerable indignation by their artificial madness. Many of the leading dadaists—Picabia, Max Ernst and Ribemont-Dessaignes, among others—held one-man shows at the Sans Pareil. Later in the year, a dada festival was held at the Salle Gaveau. The following year, 1921, was marked by the publication of *The Magnetic Fields*, a collection of automatic writings by André Breton and Philippe Soupault. In 1922, a large international exhibition was arranged by the orthodox dadaists at the Galerie Montaigne. The outcome of all these activities was the publication in

6 CAHIERS D'ART: 9no1-4:11-58 1934.

Maternity. 1924. Oil on canvas, 36 x 29 inches. Collection René Gaffé, Brussels.

Landscape. 1924–25. Oil on canvas. Collection Mme. Jacques Doucet, Paris.

The Family. 1924. Chalk drawing on glass paper, 29½ x 41 inches. Collection René Gaffé, Brussels.

1924 of the *First Manifesto of Surrealism* by André Breton, in which he gives the definition: "Surrealism, n. Pure psychic automatism, by which it is intended to express verbally, in writing or by other means, the real process of thought . . . thought's dictation, all exercise of reason and every esthetic or moral preoccupation being absent." And Miro tells us that during the year 1924–1925, "I went about a great deal with poets because I thought one must go beyond form to achieve poetry."[7]

Miro's constant aim since *The Farm* of 1922 had been the creation of a vocabulary of pictorial symbols suggestive enough to bring with them a rich overtone of extra-pictorial associations. His dadaistic *In Reverse* (page 29) marked a broad step from the *Catalan Landscape* in this direction and his *Pastoral* of 1924 (page 30) went even further in the elimination of realistic details. In *The Family* of the same year (above) we find a skeletal, symbolic anticipation of *The Harlequin's Carnival* of 1924–1925; and in *Maternity* (page 31) an even starker simplification of the central figure of *The Family*, given a quality of suggestion such as will later characterize Miro's whole production.

However, the culmination of this period of Miro's development is his *The Harlequin's Carnival*. Just as *The Farm* had summed up his efforts at objective description, *The Harlequin's Carnival* may be said to sum up his experiments in subjective description. In it we see distortions of those now familiar motives which made their first important appearance in *The Farm*: the ladder, the ear, the eye, the palette, the figure with the pipe and beard which appeared in the *Catalan Landscape* and, variously metamorphosed, in a dozen other canvases, as well as the gigantic female marionette with its dadaistic wheel tying the whole composition to its earlier, starker version in *The Family*. And now color has taken on a blithe gaiety in keeping with the marionette spirit of the

[7] MIRO, JOAN. Je rêve d'un grand atelier. xx Siècle 1no2:25-8 My 1938.

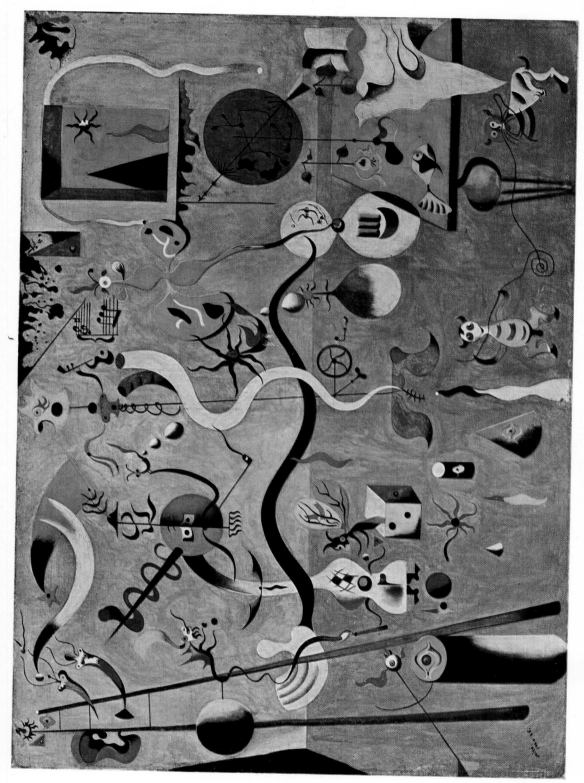

The Harlequin's Carnival. 1924–25. Oil on canvas, 26 x 36⅝ inches. Albright Art Gallery, Buffalo, New York.

THE LIBRARY
COLBY JUNIOR COLLEGE
NEW LONDON, N. H.

25690

Composition. 1925. Oil on canvas.

fantasy, quite different from its crisp severity in *The Farm*, or its vibrant sensuality in *The Tilled Field*. With the turn from the objective world to the symbolic, rhythmic interest has almost excluded the architectonic in Miro's mind. The symbolic musical staves transcribed in the upper right of *The Harlequin's Carnival* recall the word-fragment S a r d, symbol of the dance, which he had written on the *Catalan Landscape*. And the unity of the composition is now obviously dependent on the melody of its free swinging lines, rather than on the assertive bricklike or mosaic masonry of *The Farm*.

But fantasy and subjective description were not enough for Miro. He was ever more eager to exceed the limitations of his art. Surrealism pointed the way. For through surrealism's approach he saw the way to break his link with both subjective and objective description, confident that his sound technical training and essential loyalty to painting would protect him against losing sight of the fundamentally pictorial nature of his work.

1925-1927

The year 1925 saw Miro wipe his canvases practically clean in order to give a final blow to any surviving fetter of reasoned form. He felt the most drastic step possible was the only practical one toward the compassing of the surrealist ideal—the expression of "the real process of thought . . . thought's dictation, all exercise of thought's reason and every esthetic or moral preoccupation being absent." *Composition* (above) and *Glove with Face* (page 36) are two of the early steps

35

Glove with Face. 1925. Tempera and oil on canvas, 45¾ x 35 inches. The Valentine Gallery, New York.

toward a new idiom, the direction in which Miro has continued down to the present day. Descriptive forms and the fantastic distortions of them have now disappeared completely. In their place we find masses of color embodying the simplest compositional schemes, symbolic extracts of forms, a complete ideography made credible only through the artist's powerful gift of poetic suggestion.

As a consequence of the energy and enthusiasm which Miro gave to this new directive, 1926 and 1927 mark two of the richest years of his production to date. The new-found idiom seemed to exhilarate him. He undertook large canvases with as little trepidation as he had experienced in undertaking a charcoal sketch a few years earlier. And canvas after canvas shows an unwavering conviction, a consistent freedom from formal convention and a fertile spontaneity of irrational associations. The same holds true whether the subject matter is as elusive and ambiguous as his 1926 *Nude* (page 37), as naive as his *Dog Barking at the Moon* (page 38), as cyclopean as *Person Throwing a Stone at a Bird* (page 39), or as monumental as his *Portrait* (page 41). Occasionally there is a recognizable link with the work of his contemporaries, André Masson, for instance, in *Kites* (page 43). The year 1927 also saw the large circus paintings, some as schematic as *The Fratellini* (page 45), some more ideographic in the vein of *The Horse* (page 46). In his paintings of this period Miro, with almost abstract forms, achieved a lyric harmony of design and color which conveys a sense of mysterious inevitability excelled in his work perhaps only by the great compositions of 1933.

36

Nude. 1926. Oil on canvas, 36 x 28¾ inches. Collection Mr. and Mrs. Walter C. Arensberg, Hollywood.

Dog Barking at the Moon. 1926. Oil on canvas, 28¾ x 36¼ inches. Museum of Living Art, New York University, New York.

Person Throwing a Stone at a Bird. 1926. Oil on canvas, 29 x 36¼ inches. The Museum of Modern Art, New York.

Portrait. 1927. Oil on canvas, 57½ x 45 inches. Collection Mme. Helena Rubinstein, New York.

Landscape by the Sea. 1926. Oil on canvas, 29 x 36⅝ inches. Private Collection, New York.

The Kites. 1927. Oil on canvas.

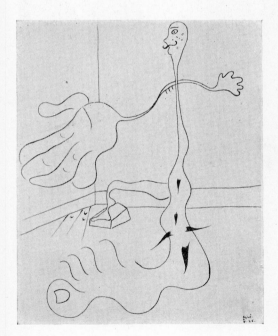

Statue. 1926. Charcoal, 24½ x 18⅜ inches.
The Museum of Modern Art, New York.

Composition. 1927. Oil on canvas, 13 x 9½ inches. Private Collection, New York.

The Lasso. 1927. Oil on canvas, 51 x 38 inches. Collection René Gaffé, Brussels.

44

The Fratellini. 1927. Oil on canvas, 51 x 38 inches. Museum of Living Art, New York University, New York.

The Horse. 1927. Oil on canvas, 51⅜ x 38¼ inches. The Chester Dale Collection, New York.

46

1928

Although Miro realized the value which a thoroughgoing conformation to the surrealist approach had for him at this time, he was not blind to the risks entailed in the surrealist method—the danger of over-simplification, of superficiality and technical slovenliness. Furthermore, he had been schooled too long in the painter's craft to be able to subscribe in more than a limited degree to the surrealist requirement that in painting, as in writing, *every* esthetic preoccupation must be absent.

In 1928 Miro made a trip to the Netherlands, and on his return produced a small number of carefully painted *Dutch Interiors* (page 48) which recall the spirit of the *Harlequin's Carnival*. It is possible that this temporary return to objective painting was a consequence of his encounter with the Dutch genre tradition. Perhaps it was merely the expression of a renewed need for the discipline of observation and descriptive painting to help him get his bearings after his two years' plunge into the world of irrationality and free association. But, just as in his pre-surrealist phases, reality was gradually submitted to fantastic distortion. And with the growth of fantastic distortion in a canvas such as the *Potato* (frontispiece), we find a much greater rhythmic freedom than Miro had achieved during the period of the *Harlequin's Carnival*. In comparison with the *Potato*, the *Harlequin's Carnival* now seems more a dance of spirochetes than a broad rhythmic organization. During the intervening years Miro's exercises in drawing from his imagination without a model had undoubtedly encouraged a more assertive gesture-rhythm than he had been able to achieve earlier. This new-found graphic freedom and assurance shows itself in the same year in a series of large drawings on felt paper (page 49), which announce the powerful calligraphy of his mature style.

1928-1933

Then, just as the pendulum had swung temporarily away from surrealist interests, toward the end of 1928 we find it swinging back again with an equal or even greater force; and after Miro's Dutch fantasies and his drawings of 1928, begin a long series of collages of sandpaper, tar, wire, feathers and wood. In these his aim was a dual one: the unusual opposition of texture and forms and through these unconventional oppositions the stimulation of surprising associations. The collage-drawing *Mercury* (page 51) shows his interest in simple contrasting textures; the *Spanish Dancer* (page 52) is rich in both the play of textures and their bizarre associations. These collages with their apparently haphazard juxtaposition of materials and objects were an expression of the surrealist poetry of accident and incongruity.

The only important paintings of 1929 were a series of imaginary portraits of which the *Portrait of Mrs. Mills in 1750* (page 50) is the richest. And in 1930 certain of Miro's constructions achieve an esthetic quality beyond any surrealist preoccupation, for example *Relief Construction* (page 51) with its simplified statement of the central biomorphic form of his 1929 oils.

Dutch Interior. 1928. Oil on canvas, 36 x 28½ inches. Bignou Gallery, New York

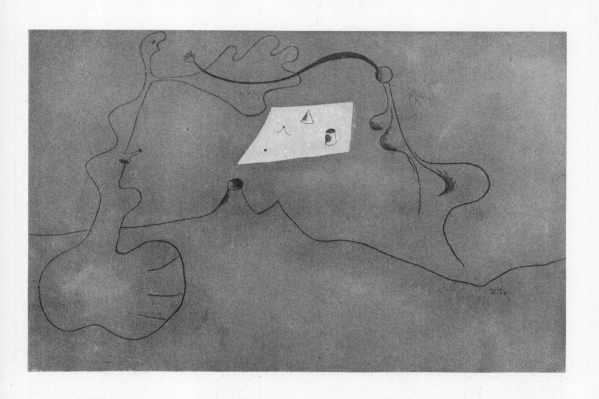

Drawing on felt paper. 1928. Collection Pierre Loeb, Paris.

Portrait of Mrs. Mills in 1750. 1929. Oil on canvas, 45½ x 35 inches. Collection Mrs. Valentine Dudensing, New York.

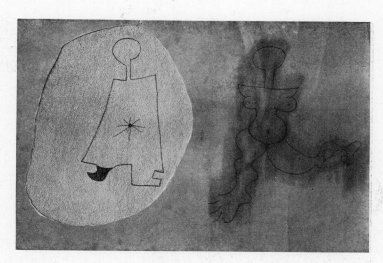

Mercury. 1929. Collage of sandpaper with drawing.

Relief Construction. 1930. Wood and metal, 35⅞ x 27⅞ inches. The Museum of Modern Art, New York.

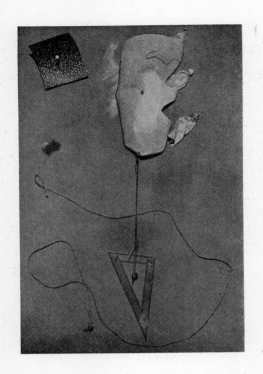

Spanish Dancer. 1930. Collage.

Watercolor. 1931.

52

In 1931 Miro carried his experiments in automatic drawing into the field of painting. He elicited suggestions from his unconscious mind in a series of watercolors (page 52). Zervos[8] states that he would begin by spilling a little color on the paper and then as his brush moved over the surface, the image would gradually take shape without any conscious direction. These watercolors point toward the broad decorative handling of the large canvases of 1933.

During the summer of 1931 he continued his researches in the field of irrational associations employing surrealist objects and constructions. These were what the surrealists described as *evénéments poétiques*—"objects functioning symbolically," in contradiction to the earlier dada "objects of concrete irrationality," (such as Duchamp's birdcage full of marble sugar-lumps entitled "*Why not Sneeze?*"). The most famous of Miro's surrealist objects, described as *Personnage*,[9] was a large wooden form about six feet high which supported an open umbrella and a paper flower. His summer was prolific of constructions in this spirit; and it was on seeing them and the earlier watercolor series of the same year that Massine was struck by the possibility of having Miro design sets and costumes for the ballet *Jeux d'Enfants* (page 84).

Work on these designs took Miro until May of 1932. He was not able to get back to painting until the summer. His first work was a group of small pictures of the type of the *Seated Woman* (page 54), painted on wood panels in extremely acid colors with a remarkable swing, assurance and strength. These pictures are clearly automatic dictations and as such are direct descendants of his watercolor experiments of 1931.

The following year, 1933, remains one of Miro's richest. In a series of large oils he combined free swinging manual rhythms, broad decorative color areas and a deep atmospheric tone. These were brought into a spiritual unity by "thought's dictation" without any explicit suggestion of reality, nor yet any feeling that subject matter is lacking. In a composition such as that on page 55, we have the complete justification of Miro's complaint against the abstract painters who invited him to enroll in their group. For here we evidently have "signs transcribed on the canvas at the moment when they correspond to a concrete reality" in Miro's mind which are infused with that reality. As a consequence they possess a convincing pictorial integrity in spite of the unfamiliarity of their symbols.

Zervos states that Miro's manner of approaching the production of these large canvases of 1933 was through a deliberate provocation of chance associations to provide him with subject matter. Miro, according to Zervos,[10] cut out a number of advertisements from newspapers, pasted them together as collages and hung them on the walls of his studio. "The forms of these collages suggested other forms to him, even as clouds often suggest fantastic images to us." Miro employed the images derived from the collage forms to set in motion a series of reflections.

[8] CAHIERS D'ART 9no1–4:18 1934.
[9] Reproduced in *Le Surréalisme au service de la Révolution*, no3 D 1931.
[10] CAHIERS D'ART 9no1–4:18 1934.

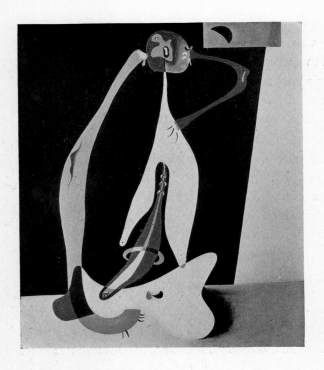

Seated Woman. 1932. Oil on wood, 18¼ x 15 inches. Pierre Matisse Gallery, New York.

These in turn endowed the images that provoked them with a rich and often extremely intimate associational life. As a result, in the eventual transcription of these visualized forms, Miro was able to give them all the intensity of the emotion his images had aroused. If we examine these forms closely we will distinguish clearly discernible sexual motives in many of the compositions; in others we recognize various elements familiar from earlier work, for example the seated dog, the ox and the horse from *The Farm*, in the large *Composition* (page 55). Nevertheless, for all this emphasis on subject matter, Miro's memory of the material character of his collage inspiration always prevented his phantasy from carrying him too far from the strictly formal. The consequence is a group of compositions surpassing in austere richness and suggestive mystery every phase of Miro's work up to that date.

In the same year, in a series of smaller collages, Miro's pursuit of associative suggestion took another turn. Instead of using collages merely as catalytics or *agents provocateurs*, Miro now varied his procedure. He began by pasting two or three postcards or banal illustrations haphazard on a blank sheet of drawing paper. He would then draw as freely as possible, allowing the subject matter, forms and relationships of the pasted bits to suggest the composition in which he gradually incorporated them.

54

Composition. 1933. Oil on canvas, 68½ x 77¼ inches. The Museum of Modern Art, New York.

Composition. 1933. Oil on canvas, 58 x 45¼ inches. Private Collection, New York.

Painting. 1933. Oil on canvas, 51½ x 64 inches. Collection Dr. and Mrs. Leslie M.
Maitland, West Los Angeles.

58

Composition. 1933. Oil on canvas, 51¼ x 64 inches. Wadsworth Atheneum, Hartford.

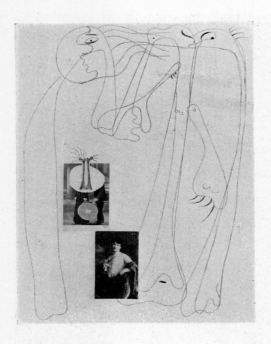

Drawing-collage. 1933. Chalk and pasted postcards, 24½ x 18½ inches. Pierre Matisse Gallery, New York.

1934-1937

All these experiments of 1933 were the direct source of his best work of the following year, such as his *The Blue Star* (page 61), and his large pastel, *The Lovers* (page 62). During 1934 this calligraphic emphasis continued to dominate Miro's work in all media with a constantly growing force and assurance. It is as if Miro through the aid of surrealism had at this point uncovered certain atavistic leanings for the decorative virtues of oriental running line, previously lost sight of with so many other associations of his Catalan boyhood. Besides this there is undoubtedly the influence of Kandinsky, whom Miro holds in high esteem. Kandinsky's emphasis on automatic drawing possibly antedates that of any other twentieth-century artist. At the same time Kandinsky had an inherent sympathy for the oriental rooted in his Russian background. One of the major tendencies of twentieth-century painting since the important exhibition of Mohammedan art in Munich in 1903 had been an effort toward the effective fusion of eastern and western pictorial idioms. This had been the basis of the complete evolution of Kandinsky's work. Beneath the greatest painting of the first romanesque style in Catalonia lay a synthesis of oriental and European strains which came together in the Mark of Hispania in that period. Consequently Kandinsky would have had a dual interest for Miro at this point. In any case, from this period to the present day we find that in Miro's work a rhythmic linearism continues to hold the ascendancy it took with the collages of 1933.

The Blue Star. 1934. Gouache and pencil on red paper, 19½ x 25½ inches. Private Collection, New York.

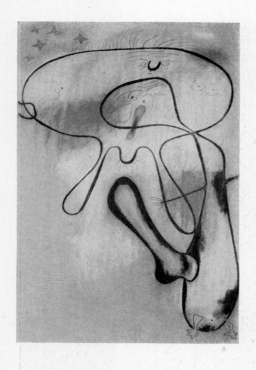

The Lovers. 1934. Pastel, 41½ x 27½ inches. Collection Mr. and Mrs. Walter C. Arensberg, Hollywood.

Another feature of his prolific experiments of 1933 was his continuing interest in textures. This is particularly noticeable in his oil paintings on sandpaper (page 63) of that year and the next. Finally in 1935 we see a combination of all three interests—the textural, the linear and the symbolic—in his series of rope and figure compositions (page 64). And these may be said to close Miro's experiments along surrealist lines to find a way to his ideal—the picture which would be rich in suggestion without employing a distracting realism.

The summer of 1936 brought a set of colorful oils on masonite panels. And in watercolors such as the *Gardener* (page 66) of the same year we have a composition of extremely personal symbols exhaling a fresh poetry through sheer delicacy of line and subtlety of placing. But whether or not the war in Spain had begun to make esthetic preoccupations difficult for Miro, the fact is that during the years 1936 and 1937 we find relatively little of that profound searching after fresh modes of expression which had characterized all his development up to the middle of 1934. And the paintings which closed 1935, such as the apocalyptic *Person in the Presence of Nature* (page 66), have a distinct nightmare cast and offered little evidence of new pictorial interests on Miro's part. Even the general tone of his 1937 work, of which the *Nursery Decoration* (page 67) painted for Henri Matisse's grandchildren is characteristic, seems to reflect a strange gloom and savagery.

Figure. 1934. Pastel, 41¾ x 27⅞
inches. Collection Mrs. Cornelius N.
Bliss, New York.

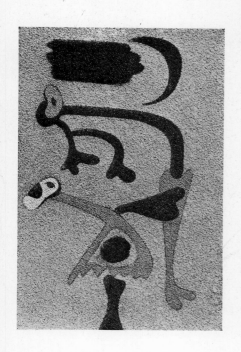

Composition. 1935. Oil on sandpaper, 14⅜ x 9¼
inches. Collection Pierre Matisse, New York.

Rope and Persons. 1935. Oil on cardboard with coil of rope, 41½ x 29½ inches. The Museum of Modern Art, New York.

Dancer. 1935. Oil and duco on cardboard, 41½ x 29¾ inches. Pierre Matisse Gallery, New York.

Tapestry, designed by Miro before 1937. 77 x 70 inches. Nierendorf Gallery, New York.

Person in the Presence of Nature. 1935. Gouache on cardboard, 29 x 41 inches. Collection Mr. and Mrs. Walter C. Arensberg, Hollywood.

The Gardener. 1936. Watercolor, 12 x 14½ inches. Collection Dr. and Mrs. Leslie M. Maitland, West Los Angeles.

Women Bathing. 1937. Oil on canvas,
5½ x 7⅛ inches. Collection Mrs. Pierre
Matisse, New York.

Nursery decoration "Pour Jackey, Peter et Pauley Matisse." 1938. Oil on canvas, 31⅜ inches x
10 feet 4 inches. Owned by Jack, Peter and Paul Matisse, New York.

Still Life with Old Shoe. 1937. Oil on canvas, 32¼ x 46¼ inches. Collection Mr. and Mrs. C. Earle Miller, Downingtown, Pa.

War, suffering and the consciousness of a separation from his home undoubtedly weighed heavily on him at this time. While Miro never had any serious political interests or affiliations, he was undoubtedly hedged in on all sides by discussions of Marxian philosophy and of class injustice. Possibly this would explain *Still Life with Old Shoe* (above), which is reminiscent in a curious way of the work of van Gogh's troubled early years. This strange isolated work was perhaps an unconscious token of his sympathy for the poverty and suffering so acute at this period in the world of his boyhood. But if his conscience was in the effort, certainly his heart was not. And in his other major production of 1937, his large mural decoration (page 69) painted on panels of masonite for the Paris Exposition of that year, we see a return to the more fantastic decorative spirit which had characterized his earlier work as a whole.

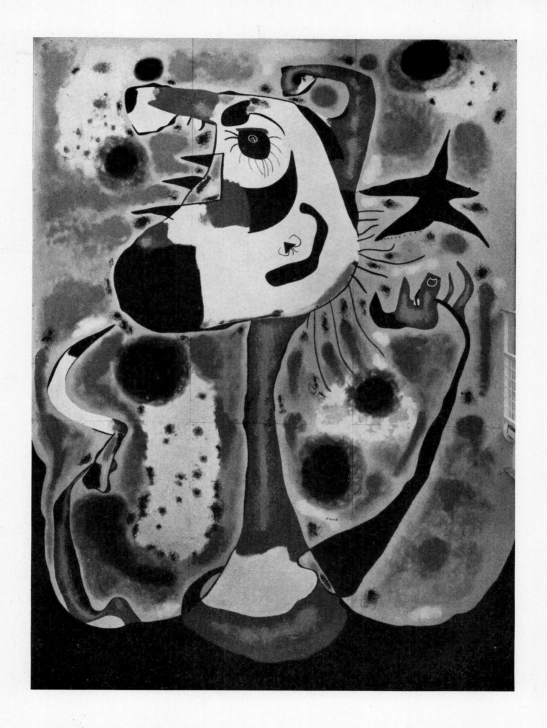

The Reaper. Mural decoration for Paris Exposition. 1937. Oil on composition board.

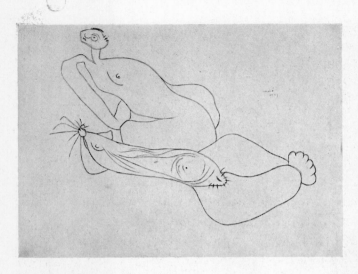

Pencil drawing. 1938. Collection Pierre Matisse, New York.

1938-1940

In 1938 with the completion of his large *Self Portrait* drawn on canvas (page 71), the burden which had been weighing on Miro for the previous two years or more seemed suddenly lifted and a new love of living began to color and liberate his work. It was as if he had made a sort of examination of conscience and a confession in the plotting of this strange illusive and complex self portrait. After his return to a relative objectivism in the *Still Life with Old Shoe*, he felt the need to look into himself and put his aims before him. And in the self portrait we have the perfect symbolic realization of Miro in his true character of naive, fantast, mischief-lover, visionary, poet and meticulous craftsman. The draughtsman was preponderantly present; the only side of Miro's character as an artist absent was his love of color. But perhaps he was so sure of that and

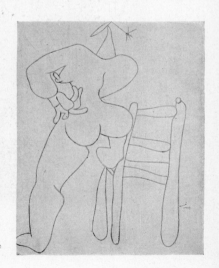

Pencil drawing. 1938. Collection Pierre Matisse, New York.

70

Self Portrait. 1938. Pencil and oil on canvas, 57½ x 38¼ inches. Collection Pierre Matisse, New York.

his unwavering loyalty to it, even in his most uncertain moments, that he did not feel it necessary here to set it down. And certainly in the paintings immediately after, his color comes out with a resonance that it has never before shown.

In *Portrait I, May 1938* (page 73), we also have a new return of suggestive associations, irrationally juxtaposed forms—a portrait whose eyes are a star and a sun, whose nose is a heart upside down, whose mouth is a butterfly, and with an equally irrational symbolization of other features in terms that have become almost conventional in Miro's idiom. But still the painting makes no concessions to conventional description. The representation is effected purely by suggestion and association, and the pictorial forms employed are clearly related to Miro's researches in the field of collage. The elements are fresh, the representation convincing, and the whole carries a quality of color unfamiliar even in Miro's strongest earlier compositions.

In his return from quasi-objective description of the *Still Life with Old Shoe* to extra-pictorial suggestions he now goes a step further, to the incorporation of written words in the picture itself, with the purpose of using them both as compositional elements on the basis of their physical forms and from a suggestive viewpoint to evoke extra-pictorial associations through their verbal significance (*Painting-poem*, page 74).

Such a device had already been anticipated to some degree by Miro in his dadaistic use of verbal fragments in his 1924 canvases. In 1925, in certain drawings he occasionally incorporated poetic images written in longhand. But now he goes further than the dadaistic hint, and we find whole phrases carried over into large decorative oils, making an intimate part of the composition. His aim, as he explained, was to fuse the pictorial and linguistic suggestions in one expression. The suggestion afforded by the pictorial element should support that contained in the verbal significance of the embodied sentence, and vice versa. The title, in this way, is taken over into the picture and, thanks to the essential calligraphic nature of Miro's style, it becomes an important pictorial factor entirely aside from the linguistic associations it may have to contribute. The whole, then, is fused into a gay unity by a bold use of contrasting colors.

Color and a poetry of formal suggestions blend again in the brilliant *Nocturne* of 1938 (page 75), even though here Miro follows a more traditional vein of pictorial suggestion than that of his large *Painting-poem* or *Portrait I*.

And finally it was color and his ceaseless search after new means for creating poetry out of visual forms that carried Miro down to the dark close of 1939 in the series of small pictures of the type of *Persons Magnetized by the Stars Walking on the Music of a Furrowed Landscape* (page 76).

Portrait 1. 1938. Oil on canvas, 64¼ x 51¼ inches. Collection Mrs. Saidie A. May, Baltimore.

Painting-poem. 1938. Oil on canvas, 51 x 76 inches. Pierre Matisse Gallery, New York.

Nocturne. 1938. Oil on compoboard, 22 x 29 inches. Private Collection, New York.

Persons Magnetized by the Stars Walking on the Music of a Furrowed Landscape. 1939. Oil on canvas, 18 x 13⅛ inches. Collection Mrs. H. Gates Lloyd, Haverford, Pa.

Women and Kite among the Constellations. 1939. Oil on burlap, 31⅞ x 23⅝ inches. Collection Mrs. George Helm, New York.

The fall of France swept Miro from Varengeville-sur-Mer, where he had lived in relative seclusion during the last year, across the border of Spain to Majorca. Since then only fragmentary news of his work has crossed the Atlantic, but always word of continued research—"Joan works now in a very minute manner, pushing the execution to an extreme. As this work represents a new step in his studies and at the same time a point of departure for new *realizations* which he has in mind . . ." (from a letter of May 14, 1941).

Tomorrow a new epoch in painting will have opened. Yesterday a period closed. But the search for new ways of expressing new things will go on. And Miro may be said to have carried on most consistently those researches which have brought western painting from the austere disciplines of cubism to new forms and new evocations.

In Miro's researches we have the reflection of a restless, unsatisfied age. But his work is not a scoffing, satirical, or defeatist expression of this period-character. It is the record of a persistent constructive effort to achieve a sound balance of the spiritual with the material in painting, an esthetic paradigm for a fuller, richer life in other fields. Disillusion and reflections on decadence have no place in it. Miro's work belongs to the youth of a period that is opening, rather than the old age of a closing one. A pictorial poetry in which oriental and occidental traditions fused was an essential part of his Catalan heritage reaching back to the Beatus illuminations of the Middle Ages. A loyalty to the traditional folk expressions of his native land has kept his feet solidly on the ground.

Miro's vitality, laughter, naive lyricism and love of life are, today, auguries of the new painting in the new period which is to come.

JAMES JOHNSON SWEENEY

APPENDICES

Catalog of the exhibition

Works by Miro illustrated in this book on pages listed below were included in the exhibition *Joan Miro*, November 18, 1941 to January 11, 1942, at the Museum of Modern Art, New York:

16, 17, 24, 25, 27, 29, 30, 33, 36, 37, 38, 39, 41, 42, 43 (bottom), 44 (top), 45, 46, 48, 50, 51 (bottom), 54, 55, 57, 58, 59, 60, 61, 62, 63, 64, 65, 66, 67, 68, 71, 73, 74, 75, 76, 77.

The following works, not illustrated in this book, were also included in the exhibition:

Glove and Newspaper. 1921. Oil on canvas, 46 x 35 inches. Collection Pierre Matisse, New York.

The Carbide Lamp. 1922–23. Oil on canvas, 15 x 18 inches. The Museum of Modern Art, New York.

Composition. 1924. Oil and pencil on wood, 7⅜ x 10¾ inches. Wadsworth Atheneum, Hartford.

Circus. 1927. Oil on canvas, 45¾ x 35¼ inches. Valentine Gallery, New York.

The Sun. 1927. Oil on burlap, 14⅞ x 18 inches. Collection Mrs. Valentine Dudensing, New York.

Dutch Interior. 1928. Oil on canvas, 50¾ x 38 inches. Collection Mme. Marie Cuttoli, New York.

Composition. 1931. Watercolor, 25 x 18½ inches. Collection Henry McBride, New York.

Object. 1932. Painted stone, shell, wood and mirror, 22 inches wide. Museum of Living Art, New York University, New York.

Composition. 1933. Oil on canvas, 45 x 57½ inches. Valentine Gallery, New York.

Drawing-collage. 1933. Chalk and pasted postcards, 24½ x 18½ inches. Pierre Matisse Gallery, New York.

Persons. 1934. Pastel and ink. 24¾ x 18½ inches. Pierre Matisse Gallery, New York.

Two figures on green paper. 1934. Ink, 27½ x 19½ inches. Pierre Matisse Gallery, New York.

Drawing on sandpaper with collage. 1934. 14½ x 9⅛ inches. Pierre Matisse Gallery, New York.

Persons Attracted by the Form of the Mountain. 1936. Tempera on board, 13 x 19¾ inches. Collection Mrs. Saidie A. May, Baltimore.

Persons. 1936. Watercolor and oil, 15⅞ x 12½ inches. Valentine Gallery, New York.

Summer. 1938. Gouache, 14 x 10½ inches. Collection Mrs. Saidie A. May, Baltimore.

Mongoose. Rug designed by Miro, 1938. 62 x 80 inches. The Museum of Modern Art, New York.

Rug designed by Miro, 1938, 6 x 4 ft; and original design for the rug, 14¾ x 9⅞ inches. Collection A. Conger Goodyear, Old Westbury, N. Y.

Woman, Flower and Star. Tapestry designed by Miro. Collection Mme. Marie Cuttoli, New York. Lent through the San Francisco Museum of Art.

Series of 17 etchings. 1939. Pierre Matisse Gallery, New York.

Paintings by Miro in American museums and private collections open to the public

A star* indicates that the item was included in the exhibition at the Museum of Modern Art, and a page reference that it is illustrated in this book. The list may not be complete. Prints are not included.

BALTIMORE, MARYLAND. THE BALTIMORE MUSEUM OF ART, COLLECTION OF MRS. SAIDIE A. MAY

    Reclining Nude. 1937. Drawing, 9 x 12 inches
    *Portrait 1. 1938. Oil, 64¼ x 51¼ inches. (page 73)
    *Summer. 1938. Gouache, 14 x 10½ inches
    A Night Scene. Watercolor and collage, 25 x 19 inches
    *Persons Attracted by the Form of a Mountain. 1936. Tempera, 13 x 19¼ inches
    Figures and Birds in a Landscape. Gouache, 11 x 19½ inches

BUFFALO, NEW YORK. ALBRIGHT ART GALLERY, BUFFALO FINE ARTS ACADEMY

    *The Harlequin's Carnival. 1924–25. Oil, 26 x 36⅝ inches (page 33)

HARTFORD, CONNECTICUT. WADSWORTH ATHENEUM

    *Composition. 1924. Oil and pencil on wood, 7⅜ x 10¾ inches
    *Composition. 1933. Oil, 51¼ x 64 inches. (page 55)
    Studies for ballet *Roméo et Juliette*, produced 1926: Curtain. 1925. Oil, 50 x 37¼ inches; Study for setting. 1925. 19 x 25 inches

MERION, PENNSYLVANIA. THE BARNES FOUNDATION

    Two Women Surrounded by Birds. 1936. Oil on paper, 19¼ x 25¼ inches
    Group of Persons. 1938. Oil, 10½ x 8½ inches
    Group of Women. 1938. Oil, 13¾ x 10¾ inches

NEW YORK. THE CHESTER DALE COLLECTION (OPEN BY APPOINTMENT ONLY)

    *The Horse. 1927. Oil, 51⅜ x 38¼ inches (page 46)

NEW YORK. MUSEUM OF LIVING ART, NEW YORK UNIVERSITY

    *Dog Barking at the Moon. 1926. Oil, 28¾ x 36¼ inches (page 38)
    Painting. 1926. Oil, 8¼ x 10¼ inches
    *The Fratellini. 1927. Oil, 51 x 38 inches (page 45)
    *Object. 1932. Painted stone, shell, wood, mirror, 22 inches wide
    Painting. 1933. Oil, 51 x 64 inches
    Painting. 1934. Oil and paper on sandpaper, 14¼ x 9¼ inches

NEW YORK. THE MUSEUM OF MODERN ART

    Landscape. (c.1916). Oil on cardboard, 32½ x 20½ inches
    *The Ear of Grain. 1922–23. Oil, 14⅞ x 18⅛ inches (page 24)
    *The Carbide Lamp. 1922–23. Oil, 15 x 18 inches
    *Catalan Landscape (The Hunter). 1923–24. Oil, 25½ x 39½ inches (page 29)
    *Statue. 1926. Charcoal, 24½ x 18⅜ inches (page 43)
    *Person Throwing a Stone at a Bird. 1926. Oil, 29 x 36¼ inches (page 39)
    Portrait of a Lady in 1820. 1929. Oil, 45¾ x 35⅛ inches

*Relief Construction. 1930. Wood and metal, 35⅞ x 27⅜ inches (page 51)

*Composition. 1933. Oil, 68½ x 77¼ inches (page 55)

*Rope and Persons. 1935. Oil on cardboard with coil of rope, 41½ x 29½ inches (page 64)

SAN DIEGO, CALIFORNIA. FINE ARTS GALLERY, COLLECTION MRS. SAIDIE A. MAY

Two Persons. Gouache, 18 x 24½ inches

Exhibitions of Miro's Work

1918 BARCELONA. *Galerie Dalmau.*
Feb. 16 to Mar. 3.

1921 PARIS. *Galerie La Licorne.*
Apr. 29 to May 14. Organized by M. Dalmau, sponsored by Maurice Raynal.

1923 PARIS. *Caméléon Club.*
September.

1925 PARIS. *Galerie Pierre.*
June 12 to 27. Organized by Jacques Viot. (In Nov. 1925 Miro exhibited in first collective exhibition of the surrealist group, Galerie Pierre.)

1928 PARIS. *Galerie Georges Bernheim et Cie.*
May 1 to 15. Organized by the Galerie Pierre.

1929 BRUSSELS. *Galerie Le Centaure.*
May 11 to 23.

1930 PARIS. *Galerie Pierre.*
May 7 to 22.

1930 NEW YORK. *The Valentine Gallery.*
Oct. 13 to Nov. 1.

1931 CHICAGO. *The Arts Club of Chicago.*
Jan. 27 to Feb. 17.

1931 PARIS. *Galerie Pierre.*
Dec. 18, 1931 to Jan. 8, 1932.

1931 NEW YORK. *The Valentine Gallery.*
Dec. 18, 1931 to Jan. 8, 1932.

1932 NEW YORK. *Pierre Matisse Gallery.*
Nov. 1 to 25.

1932 PARIS. *Galerie Pierre Colle.*
Dec. 13 to 16.

1933 LONDON. *The Mayor Gallery.*
July.

1933 PARIS. *Galerie Georges Bernheim et Cie.*
Oct. 30 to Nov. 13. Organized by the Galerie Pierre.

1933 NEW YORK. *Pierre Matisse Gallery.*
Dec. 29, 1933 to Jan. 18, 1934.

1934 CHICAGO. *The Arts Club of Chicago.*
Mar. 16 to 30.

1934 PARIS. *Galerie des Cahiers d'Art.*
May 3 to 19. Organized by Yvonne Zervos.

1934 SAN FRANCISCO. *East-West Gallery.*
June. Organized by Howard Putzel.

1935 NEW YORK. *Pierre Matisse Gallery.*
Jan. 10 to Feb. 9.

1935 SAN FRANCISCO. *San Francisco Museum of Art.* June 30 to Aug. 12, and Dec. 1 to 15.

1935 LOS ANGELES. *Stendahl Gallery.*
September.

1935 HOLLYWOOD. *Stanley Rose Gallery.*
October. Organized by Howard Putzel.

1936 NEW YORK. *Pierre Matisse Gallery.*
Nov. 30 to Dec. 26.

1937 HOLLYWOOD. *Siegel Antheil Gallery.*
March.

1937 HOLLYWOOD. *Putzel Gallery.*
March.

82

1937 LONDON. *The Zwemmer Gallery.*
May 6 to June 2.

1937 HONOLULU. *Honolulu Academy of Arts.*
Summer.

1938 NEW YORK. *Pierre Matisse Gallery.*
Apr. 18 to May 7.

1938 CHICAGO. *Katherine Kuh Galleries.*
Nov. 1 to 30.

1939 LONDON. *London Gallery* (with Louis
Marcoussis). Apr. 14 to 27. Organized
by E. L. T. Mesens.

1939 NEW YORK. *Pierre Matisse Gallery.*
Apr. 10 to May 6.

1940 NEW YORK. *Pierre Matisse Gallery.*
Mar. 1 to Apr. 10.

1941 NEW YORK. *Pierre Matisse Gallery.*
Mar. 4 to 29.

1941 NEW YORK. *The Museum of Modern Art.*
Nov. 18, 1941 to Jan. 11, 1942.

Prints by Miro

ETCHINGS

1939 Suite of 17 etchings.

1935 One etching in portfolio edited by Anatole Jakovski, Paris, G. Orobitz et Cie.

COLOR LITHOGRAPHS

1937 Verve 1no1:10 D ("The Four Elements:
Air")

1938 Verve 1no3:99 O-D ("Summer").

COLOR STENCILS (*pochoirs*)

1934 Cahiers d'Art 9no1–4:19, 37.

1934 D'Aci i d'Allà (Barcelona) 22no179:56.

1937 Cahiers d'Art 12no4–5:[155]

COLOR WOODCUTS

1938 XX siècle no4:[45].

MAGAZINE COVERS

1935 Minotaure no7.

1936 Transition no25.

1940 Cahiers d'Art 15no3–4.

Books illustrated by Miro

FOIX, J. V. Gertrudis. Barcelona, L'Amic de les
Arts.
See bibliography 27 & 18, where this title is listed
without date.

———— Krtu. Barcelona, L'Amic de les Arts.
See bibliography 27 & 18, where this title is listed
without date.

HIRTZ, LISE. Il était une petite pie. Paris,
Bucher, 1928. Color stencils.

HUGNET, GEORGES. Enfances. Paris, Cahiers
d'Art, 1935. Etchings.

PAALEN, ALICE. Sablier couché. Paris, Editions
Sagesse, 1938. Etchings.

PÉRET, BENJAMIN. Et les seins mouraient. Mar-
seilles, Cahiers du Sud, 1928. Frontispiece: line-
cut of drawing.

SINDREU, CARLES. Darrera el vidre. Barcelona,
L'Amic de les Arts.
See bibliography 18, where this title is listed without
date.

TZARA, TRISTAN. L'arbre des voyageurs. Paris,
Editions Montaigne, 1930. Lithographs.

UBU ENCHAINÉ. Paris, Imprimerie de Rocroy
1937.
Pamphlet issued with the production of Alfred
Jarry's play by the Compagnie du Diable Ecarlate,
September 22–26, 1937. Illustrations from original
drawings by Miro and other artists.

Ballets in which Miro collaborated

ROMÉO ET JULIETTE
Ballet in two tableaux. Music: Constant Lambert. Scenery: Joan Miro and Max Ernst. Choreography: Bronia Nijinska. First produced: Théâtre de Monte Carlo, May 4, 1926.

JEUX D'ENFANTS
Ballet in one act. Book: Boris Kochno. Music: Georges Bizet. Curtain, scenery and costumes: Joan Miro. Choreography: Léonide Massine. First produced: Théâtre de Monte Carlo, April 14, 1932.

The ballet, *Jeux d'Enfants*, with setting and costumes designed by Miro. Produced in 1932.

Bibliography

The arrangement of this bibliography is alphabetical, under the author's name wherever possible. Catalogs of exhibitions in public museums are listed under the name of the city where the museum is located, while private exhibition galleries are listed under the name of the gallery. Entries marked * are the more important essays. The bibliographical form is modelled upon that used in the Art Index.

ABBREVIATIONS. Ap *April*, Ag *August*, D *December*, ed *editor*, F *February*, Ja *January*, Je *June*, Jl *July*, Mr *March*, My *May*, N *November*, no *number*, O *October*, p *page(s)*, S *September*.

SAMPLE ENTRY for magazine article. DUTHUIT, GEORGES. Où allez vous, Miro? Cahiers d'Art 11 no8–10:261–64 1936.

EXPLANATION. An article entitled "Où allez-vous, Miro?" by Georges Duthuit, will be found in Cahiers d'Art, volume 11, number 8–10, pages 261 through 264, inclusive, 1936.

ANTHEIL, GEORGE. See 6.

1. ARAGON, LOUIS. La peinture au défi. Paris, Galerie Goemans, 1930.
   Preface to an exhibition of collages by Miro and other artists.

BARR, ALFRED H. JR. See 42–43.

2. BATAILLE, GEORGES. Joan Miro: peintures recèntes. Documents no7:399 1930.

3. BOSSCHÈRE, JEAN DE. Notes sur la peinture et Miro. Variétés (Brussels) 1:132–9 Jl 15 1928.

4. BRETON, ANDRÉ. Le surréalisme et la peinture. Paris, Gallimard, 1928.

5. ———— What is surrealism? London, Faber & Faber, 1936.
   A translation of Qu'est-ce que le surr'alisme? Paris, Henriquez, 1934.

*6. CAHIERS D'ART 9no1–4:11–58 1934.
   Special number: "L'oeuvre de Joan Miro de 1917 à 1933." Essays by Christian Zervos, Maurice Raynal, Robert Desnos, Benjamin Péret, Ernest Hemingway, René Gaffé, Ragnar Hoppe, George Antheil, Will Grohmann, Vicente Huidobro, Pierre Guéguen, James Johnson Sweeney, Léonide Massine, Herbert Read, J. V. Foix, Jacques Viot, Anatole Jakovski.

*7. CAHIERS DE BELGIQUE 2:202–5 1929.
   Special issue, with essays by Sebastià Gasch, Robert Desnos and Salvador Dali.

8. CASSANYES, M. A. Joan Miro, el extraordinario. A.C. (Barcelona) no18:40–41 1935.

DALI, SALVADOR. See 7.

9. DAVIDSON, M. Subconscious pictography by Joan Miro. Art News 35:11 D 5 1936.

DESNOS, ROBERT. See 6–7.

10. DUTHUIT, GEORGES. Où allez vous, Miro? Cahiers d'Art 11no8–10:261–64 1936.

11. EINSTEIN, CARL. Die kunst des 20. jahrhunderts. 3. auflage. Berlin, Propyläen-Verlag, 1931.

12. ———— Joan Miro: papiers collés à la Galerie Pierre. Documents 2no4: 241–3 1930.

13. ELUARD, PAUL. Joan Miro [poem]. *In his* Capitale de la douleur. p133 Paris, Gallimard, 1926.

14. ———— Naissances de Miro. Cahiers d'Art 12no1–3:78–83 1937.

15. Enquête. Cahiers d'Art 14no1–4:73 1939.

16. Exposition Miro de sculptures-objets. Cahiers d'Art 6no9–10:431 1931.

FOIX, J. V. See 6.

17. FREY, J. G. Miro and the surrealists. Parnassus 8:13–15 O 1936.

*18. GACETA DE ARTE (Tenerife, Canary Islands) no38:5–22 Je 1936.
   "Joan Miro y la polémica de las realidades" by Eduardo Westerdahl, p6–11; criticism by Ragnar Hoppe, Vicente Huidobro, Leonide Massine and Christian Zervos; portrait, illustrations, list of one-man exhibitions, bibliography.

GAFFÉ, RENÉ. See 6.

19. GALERIE PIERRE, PARIS. Exposition Joan Miro. Je 12–27 1925.
    Catalog, containing text "Les cheveux dans les yeux" by Benjamin Péret.

20. GASCH, SEBASTIÀ. Joan Miro. Gaseta de les Arts (Barcelona) 2:63–4 Mr 1929.
    ———— See also 7.

21. GASCOYNE, DAVID. A short survey of surrealism. London, Cobden-Sanderson, 1935.

22. GRIGSON, GEOFFREY. The arts today. London, Lane, 1935.
    GROHMANN, WILL. See 6.
    GUÉGUEN, PIERRE. See 6.
    HEMINGWAY, ERNEST. See 6.

23. HENRY, MAURICE. Joan Miro. Cahiers d'Art 10no5–6:115–16 1935.

24. HILDEBRAND, HANS. Die kunst des XIX. und XX. jahrhunderts. Wildpark-Potsdam, Akademische Verlagsgesellschaft Athenaion [copyright 1924; postscript 1931].
    HOPPE, RAGNAR. See 6, 18.

25. HUGNET, GEORGES. Joan Miro; ou L'enfance de l'art. Cahiers d'Art 6no7–8:335–40 1931.

26. ———— Joan Miro [poem]. Cahiers d'Art 15no3–4:48 1940.
    ———— See also 43.
    HUIDOBRO, VICENTE. See 6, 18.

27. HUYGHE, RENÉ, ed. Histoire de l'art contemporain. Paris, Alcan, 1935.
    Biographical and bibliographical notice, p344. Originally published in L'Amour de l'Art 15:344 Mr 1934.

28. JAKOVSKI, ANATOLE. Six essais. Paris, Povolovsky, n.d.
    ———— See also 6.

29. JOAN MIRO. Cahiers d'Art 6no9–10:424–6 1931.

30. LARREA, JUAN. Miroir d'Espagne; à propos du "Faucheur" de Miro, au Pavillon espagnol de l'Exposition 1937. Cahiers d'Art 12no4–5:157–9 1937.

31. LEIRIS, MICHEL. Joan Miro. Documents no5:263–6 O 1929.

32. LUCERNE. KUNSTMUSEUM. Thèse, antithèse, synthèse. F 24–Mr 31 1935.
    Exhibition catalog; biographical and bibliographical notes.

33. MCBRIDE, HENRY. Modern art. Dial 85:541–2 D 1928.

34. MANGEOT, GUY. Histoire du surréalisme. Bruxelles, Henriquez, 1934.

35. MARRIOTT, CHARLES. A key to modern painting. London, Blackie, 1938.
    MASSINE, LEONIDE. See 6, 18.

36. MATISSE, PIERRE, GALLERY, NEW YORK. Joan Miro; exhibition of early paintings, from 1918 to 1925. Mr 12–31 1940.
    Catalog with text "I dream of a large studio" by Miro.

37. ———— Joan Miro, 1933–1934, paintings, tempera, pastels. Ja 10–F 9 1935.
    Exhibition catalog with biographical text.

*38. MIRO, JOAN. I dream of a large studio. In: Pierre Matisse Gallery, New York. Joan Miro; exhibition of early paintings. 1940.
    Translated by James Johnson Sweeney. Originally published as Je rêve d'un grand atelier, in XX Siècle 1no2:25–8 My 1938.

39. ———— [Note under color illustration of Harlequin's Carnival.] Verve no4:85 Ja-Mr 1939.
    ———— See also 54.

40. Miro's sculpture. Formes no21:210 Ja 1932.

41. MIZUÉ (Tokio) 1937.
    Special issue of the periodical, with title "Album surr´aliste," edited by Shuzo Takiguchi and Tiroux Yamanaka.

*42. NEW YORK. THE MUSEUM OF MODERN ART. Cubism and abstract art. 1937.
Text by Alfred H. Barr, Jr. Biographical and bibliographical notes.

43. ——— Fantastic art, dada, surrealism. 2d ed. 1937.
Edited by Alfred H. Barr, Jr. "In the light of surrealism," by Georges Hugnet, originally published in Bulletin of the Museum of Modern Art 4no2–3:19–32 N–D 1936. Biographical and bibliographical notes.

44. OLIVER, PERE. Joan Miro . . . exposició . . . à cân Dalmau. Vell i Nou (Barcelona) 4:89–98 Mr 1 1918.

45. OZENFANT, AMEDÉE. Foundations of modern art. New York, Brewer, Warren and Putnam, 1931.
A translation of Art. Paris, Budry, 1928.

PÉRET, BENJAMIN. See 6, 19.

46. Pour un portrait gravé de Miro, Miro et Marcoussis collaborent. Beaux-Arts p4 Je 23 1939.

47. RAYNAL, MAURICE. Modern French painters. New York, Brentano, 1928.
A translation of Anthologie de la peinture en France de 1906 à nos jours. Paris, Editions Montaigne, 1927.

——— See also 6.

48. READ, HERBERT. Art now. New York, Harcourt, Brace, 1934.

——— See also 6.

49. SACHS, MAURICE. The decade of illusion; Paris 1918–1928. New York, Knopf, 1933.

50. SINDREU, CARLES. Joan Miro. D'Aci i d'Allà (Barcelona) 22no179:56 1934.
Illustrated with color stencil made by Miro especially for the periodical.

51. SOBY, JAMES THRALL. After Picasso. Hartford, Mitchell; New York, Dodd, Mead, 1935.

52. SWEENEY, JAMES JOHNSON. Miro and Dali. New Republic 81:360 F 6 1935.

53. ——— Plastic redirections in XXth century painting. Univ. of Chicago Press, 1934.

——— See also 6, 38.

TAKIGUCHI, SHUZO. See 41.

54. TÉRIADE, E. Emancipation de la peinture. Minotaure no3–4:9–20 1934.
Includes remarks by Miro on his painting.

55. ——— Documentation sur la jeune peinture. IV: La réaction littéraire. Cahiers d'Art 5no2:69–90 1930.

56. TODD, RUTHVEN. For Joan Miro [poem]. London Bulletin no13:10 Ap 15 1939.

57. TZARA, TRISTAN. À propos de Joan Miro. Cahiers d'Art 15no3–4:37–47 1940.

58. VIOT, JACQUES. Un ami, Joan Miro. Cahiers d'Art 11no8–10:257–60 1936.

——— See also 6.

59. WATSON, PETER. Joan Miro. Horizon (London) 4no20:133 1941.

WESTERDAHL, EDUARDO. See 18.

YAMANAKA, TIROUX. See 41.

60. ZERVOS, CHRISTIAN. Histoire de l'art contemporain. Paris, Editions Cahiers d'Art, 1938.

61. ——— La nouvelle generation. Cahiers d'Art 1no9–10:379 1926.

——— See also 6, 18.

EIGHT THOUSAND COPIES OF THIS BOOK HAVE BEEN PRINTED IN NOVEMBER 1941
FOR THE TRUSTEES OF THE MUSEUM OF MODERN ART BY THE PLANTIN PRESS,
NEW YORK.

171